ideals
CHRISTMAS

D0791496

Some say that ever 'gainst that season comes
Wherein our Saviour's birth is celebrated,
The bird of dawning singeth all night long:
And then, they say, no spirit dare stir abroad,
The nights are wholesome, then no planets strike,
No fairy takes nor witch hath power to charm,
So hallow'd and so gracious is the time.

William Shakespeare
Hamlet, Act 1, Scene 1

ISBN 0-8249-1039-7 350

Publisher, Patricia A. Pingry
Editor/Ideals, Dorothy L. Gibbs
Managing Editor, Marybeth Owens
Photographic Editor, Gerald Koser
Research Editor, Linda Robinson
Editorial Assistant, Carmen Johnson
Editorial Assistant, Amanda Barrickman
Phototypesetter, Kim Kaczanowski
Art Director, Patrick McRae
Staff Artist, David Lenz

IDEALS — Vol. 42, No. 8 November MCMLXXXV IDEALS (ISSN 0019-137X) is published eight times a year,
February, March, May, June, August, September, November, December
by IDEALS PUBLISHING CORPORATION, Nelson Place at Elm Hill Pike, Nashville, Tenn. 37214
Second class postage paid at Nashville, Tennessee and additional mailing offices.
Copyright © MCMLXXXV by IDEALS PUBLISHING CORPORATION.
POSTMASTER: Send address changes to Ideals, Post Office Box 148000, Nashville, Tenn. 37214
All rights reserved. Title IDEALS registered U.S. Patent Office.
Published simultaneously in Canada.

SINGLE ISSUE — $3.50
ONE YEAR SUBSCRIPTION — eight consecutive issues as published — $15.95
TWO YEAR SUBSCRIPTION — sixteen consecutive issues as published — $27.95
Outside U.S.A., add $4.00 per subscription year for postage and handling

The cover and entire contents of IDEALS are fully protected by copyright and must
not be reproduced in any manner whatsoever. Printed and bound in U.S.A.
by The Banta Co., Menasha, Wisconsin.

Front and Back Covers
O HOLY NIGHT by American folk artist, Linda Nelson Stocks is available in a limited print edition
through The Lang Folk Art Collection at P.O. Box 99, Delafield, Wisconsin 53018 (414-646-2211)

Words for Christmas

I sought for something new to say
About the joy of Christmas Day.
The season's inspiration ought
To make my words profound, I thought;

But it's been said so many ways —
In poetry and songs of praise,
By Gospel story — paintings, too,
From towering steeples. Oh, I knew

I had no bright new words to say
About the joy of Christmas Day.
So, "Merry Christmas" everyone!
With blessings may your cup o'er run.

May all the earth heed once again
The song of "Peace, Good Will to Men."

Edna L. Furguson

Photo Opposite
CHRISTMAS GREETINGS
Fred Sieb

Postcards of Christmas Past

Exchanging Christmas greetings has been popular in the United States since the 1880's, but not until the turn of the century did Americans discover that colorful postcards were a wonderful way to extend those greetings. The initial popularity of Christmas cards encouraged publishers to produce a great variety. Some, produced between 1906 and the early 1920's, have become treasured works of art that thoughtful collectors across the country still delight in displaying.

Of course Christmas cards did not originate in America. They were flourishing in Europe as early as the 1840's. It was England where, in 1843, Sir Henry Cole first commissioned artist John Horsley to create some illustrated holiday greetings. Reportedly, about 1,000 cards were sold to the public at one shilling each. The notion found its way to America in the 1860's but was not generally accepted until Louis Prang, a German immigrant, perfected the process of lithographic color printing in the late 1870's.

Although they depended mostly on floral designs to illustrate their messages, the early cards published by Prang were considered to be of the finest quality and craftsmanship. Eventually Prang, and others, produced more conventional Christmas scenes including the Madonna and Child in the stable, evergreen trees, blazing fireplaces, and Santa Claus.

It was, perhaps, on Christmas postcards that changes in the character and costume of Santa Claus were best documented. On early cards, it wasn't at all unusual to find Santa in a purple outfit, a brown robe, or a green coat. Over the years, however, St. Nicholas, Kris Kringle, Sinterklass, Father Christmas, and Santa Claus all became one single, jolly, plump fellow in a red suit. Many holiday historians credit the American Christmas postcard, along with Clement Clarke Moore's *The Night Before Christmas* and Thomas Nast's drawings, with centralizing the image of Santa Claus and his fabled sleigh.

The era of Christmas postcards gave birth to many still-admired works of American artists, such as Helen Clapsaddle, and postcard publishers, like Raphael Tuck. The high quality of some of these postcards makes them eagerly sought by many collectors today. Also of interest are the postcards that bear hand-written messages from the early days. The messages offer a rare look into the thoughts of that generation of Americans. On a 1911 card, for example, the sender wrote, "I got a ring for Xmas. You ought to have been here and went (sic) to the Xmas tree." On another, dated 1910, was the message, "Stanley, may you live to see many a merry Christmas and no mumps, your neighbor E. C."

The postcards of Christmas past still emerge occasionally at antique shops, flea markets, and collectors' shows; once sold for a cent or two, they are valued today at from one to ten dollars. But in the past sixty years, the Christmas postcards have given way to greeting cards as we know them; and, while those colorful little postcards attracted holiday well-wishers by the millions, our modern versions are counted in the billions.

Robert Reed

When Winter Came to Call

A silver world was all about
When I awoke this morn,
For overnight the silver frost
Of winter came along.

An ermine robe was draped around
The stately evergreens,
And tatted lace of frost was placed
On frozen pond and stream.

The meadow lay in silence,
While over all the snow,
Wildlings tracked their calling cards,
Where e'er they'd come and go.

The little brook was silent,
Locked in winter's clasp,
Hemmed in crystal stitchery
With icy blades of grass.

A wondrous cloak of whiteness
The snow king laid o'er all,
Fashioned from a leaden sky
When winter came to call.

Mildred L. Jarrell

Photo Opposite
SNOWY WILLOW
Larry Lefever
Grant Heilman Photography

Sights, Sounds, and Smells

Tinsel and holly and mistletoe,
Pine trees and snowmen, faces aglow;
The smell of cookies fresh from the oven;
The spirit of joy and peace and loving;

The voices of carolers, clear on the air;
Snowflakes and angels, bells everywhere;
The bustle of shoppers with packages bright;
Shimmering icicles glistening at night;

Fruitcakes baking and holiday pies;
The laughter of children with stars in their eyes;
Santa and sleighbells and reindeer that fly,
Plum pudding and eggnog — friends dropping by,

These are the sights, smells, and sounds
    of the season;
But pause for a moment, remember the reason.

Carol Frye

It All Adds Up
to Christmas

Candy canes and lustrous holly
Mark this season of the year;
Snowy landscapes and quaint sleigh bells
Add a feeling of good cheer.

Greeting cards in great abundance,
Christmas trees with candle-shine
Bring the very best of wishes
To the folks, both yours and mine.

Mistletoe and Christmas wrappings,
Tiny shiny silver bells
Speak the message of glad Christmas,
Peace on earth, good will they tell.

Choirs of little children singing,
Joyfully the carols clear;
All of it adds up to Christmas
This glad season of the year.

Georgia B. Adams

Dreanleaf
CHRISTMAS CANDLES
H. Armstrong Roberts

Readers' Reflections

Christmas Clocks

What happens to our clocks each year
At Christmastime or near it?
Do they get too much Christmas cheer
Or just the Christmas spirit?

The clocks that were, the whole year
   through,
Dependable and steady
Tick hours off like mad when you
Have Christmas to get ready.

Yet, strange to say, those very clocks
Delight in hesitating;
They go to sleep between their tocks
When you are young and waiting.

Ruth Van Gorder
Lake Ariel, Pennsylvania

Snow Star

While walking down a lonely street,
My footsteps tired and slow,
There fell upon my jacket sleeve
A pointed flake of snow.

In all its gentle loveliness,
The perfect crystal lay
Like a star for just a moment.
Then it blurred and slipped away,

But beauty lingered in its place.
My feet fell light as on I trod
Because I held, just for a breath,
A little star from God.

Mary E. Wood
Greenwood, Indiana

The First Christmas

An angel on that holy night
Came down to earth in splendor bright
To tell the shepherds on the hill
Of peace on earth, to men good will.

While heavenly music filled the air
And wisemen offered gifts most rare,
The holy Babe there sweetly lay,
Enthroned upon a bed of hay.

Ruth Ulrich Fransen
Mesa, Arizona

Editor's Note: Readers are invited to submit poetry, short anecdotes, and humorous reflections on life for possible publication in future *Ideals* issues. Please send xeroxed copies only; manuscripts will not be returned. Writers will receive $10 for each published submission. Send materials to "Readers' Reflections." Ideals Publishing Corporation, Nelson Place at Elm Hill Pike, Nashville, Tennessee 37214.

Christmas Love to You

I've nothing else to offer,
So, to you, it's love I'll send.
It's nothing that I borrowed,
And it's nothing that I'd lend.

It has no dollar value,
And it can't be overused;
It isn't fragile, so can't break,
Though, often, it's abused.

I've given it to others,
But each time it's unique.
Its meaning's always different;
It depends on what you seek.

It's something you can store away
To feel when you're in need,
But never is it on display;
Its beauty can't be seen.

I'm giving it "no strings attached,"
No costly warranty.
This love that I am sending
Has a lifetime guarantee.

Penny Reuter
Granton, Wisconsin

Ice-skating Time

The river's frozen. Come out! Come Out!
It's skating time without a doubt.

Find some wood and build a fire
Right beside the ice.
Now it's burning; sparks are flying.
Doesn't it feel nice?

With your partner, whirling, turning,
Glide across the ice so fast,
Waltzing, dancing — oh, what fun!
How long can we make it last?

Bonfire's dying; daylight's fading.
Everyone, back home we'll go;
Cookies and hot chocolate waiting.
Oh! We love the ice and snow.

Edna Cowan
Inman, Kansas

`Midst Balsam Boughs

'Midst balsam boughs and candlelight,
With faces all aglow,
We sit beside a cheery fire
And sing the songs we know.

All join in for "Silent Night,"
And "Deck the Halls" rings clear;
They seem to make this holy night
A bit more near and dear.

The magic of a violin
Brings out the strains divine,
A wondrous sense of peace stcals
Into your heart and mine.

'Midst balsam boughs and candlelight,
We greet this day anew
And wish all those who read these lines
A "Merry Christmas," too!

Georgia B. Adams

Photo Opposite
CHRISTMAS MUSIC
Bob Taylor

Flower of the Holy Night

Far off in a mountain hamlet,
In years long, long ago...
So thus began the story
I heard in Mexico.

A little child crept softly
With a gift of weeds to lay
At the Christ Child's feet — her offering
To Him for Christmas Day.

It was evening in the chapel,
But before the morning light,
The weeds burst forth in glory
"The Flower of the Holy Night."

So the crimson bloom, "Poinsettia,"
Of the legend is today
A sign of Christmas sharing
From a child who knelt to pray.

Della Adams Leitner

Photo Opposite
POINSETTIA
Gene Ahrens

Christmas Hash *by Ogden Nash*

You wish those jingle bells would hush,
You slither through the slop and slush,
And busses spatter you with mush —
Shop counters teem with offerings lush,
You lose the sales clerk in the crush,
The world has lost its rosy flush —
That's what we call the Christmas rush —
Yes, everyone complains and hollers,
But we wouldn't miss it for a million dollars!

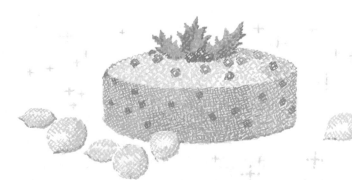

My fingers ache from lugging parcels,
I limp on battered metatarsals,
My tongue is dry from licking stamps,
I'm lost in Christmas lights and amps,
I'm in that yearly Yuletide mess,
And so are you, I shrewdly guess.
It's tough on you and rough on me
But gosh, it's worth it, don't you agree?

It's time to decorate the tree
And if you're anything like me
When you mix little bulbs and wires
Electricity expires —
Birds and stars become unspangled
Angels in your hair get tangled
And if you laugh off such mishaps
Ladders under you collapse —
But still I know if you're like me
You wouldn't miss it — no sirree!

I fear that I shall never more see
A good old-fashioned Christmas tree,
A Christmas tree of natural green
That smells so crisp and cold and clean,
The march of science is relentless,
Now trees are pink and purple and scentless,
But I prefer that ancient hue,
An evergreen Christmas — don't you?

Scrooge was a Christmas-hating miser;
It took a ghost to make him wiser.
But you and I and Tiny Tim
Are miles and miles ahead of him.
We do not need to have a ghost
Teach us a cheery Christmas toast.
And so, no sooner said than done —
My friend, God bless us, every one!

Reprinted by permission of Curtis Brown, Ltd., New York. Copyright 1959 by
Ogden Nash.

Overleaf
WINTER IN PENNSYLVANIA
James R. Cooper
(Photo, Three Lions)

Christmas Trees

The city had withdrawn into itself
And left at last the country to the country;
When between whirls of snow not come to lie
And whirls of foliage not yet laid, there drove
A stranger to our yard, who looked the city,
Yet did in country fashion in that there
He sat and waited till he drew us out,
A-buttoning coats, to ask him who he was.
He proved to be the city come again
To look for something it had left behind
And could not do without and keep its Christmas.
He asked if I would sell my Christmas trees;
My woods — the young fir balsams like a place
Where houses all are churches and have spires.
I hadn't thought of them as Christmas trees.
I doubt if I was tempted for a moment

To sell them off their feet to go in cars
And leave the slope behind the house all bare,
Where the sun shines now no warmer than the moon.
I'd hate to have them know it if I was.
Yet more I'd hate to hold my trees, except
As others hold theirs or refuse for them,
Beyond the time of profitable growth —
The trial by market everything must come to.
I dallied so much with the thought of selling.
Then whether from mistaken courtesy
And fear of seeming short of speech, or whether
From hope of hearing good of what was mine,
I said, "There aren't enough to be worth while."

"I could soon tell how many they would cut,
You let me look them over."

Madelyn Stanchfield Trebilcock

"You could look.
But don't expect I'm going to let you have them."
Pasture they spring in, some in clumps too close
That lop each other of boughs, but not a few
Quite solitary and having equal boughs
All round and round. The latter he nodded "Yes" to,
Or paused to say beneath some lovelier one,
With a buyer's moderation, "That would do."
I thought so too, but wasn't there to say so.
We climbed the pasture on the south, crossed over,
And came down on the north.

                    He said, "A thousand."

"A thousand Christmas trees! — at what apiece?"

He felt some need of softening that to me:
"A thousand trees would come to thirty dollars."

Then I was certain I had never meant
To let him have them. Never show surprise!
But thirty dollars seemed so small beside
The extent of pasture I should strip, three cents
(For that was all they figured out apiece) —
Three cents so small beside the dollar friends
I should be writing to within the hour
Would pay in cities for good trees like those,
Regular vestry-trees whole Sunday Schools
Could hang enough on to pick off enough.

A thousand Christmas trees I didn't know I had!
Worth three cents more to give away than sell,
As may be shown by a simple calculation.
Too bad I couldn't lay one in a letter.
I can't help wishing I could send you one
In wishing you herewith a Merry Christmas.

                              Robert Frost

From THE POETRY OF ROBERT FROST edited by Edward Connery Lathem. Copyright 1916, © 1969 by Holt, Rinehart and Winston. Copyright 1944 by Robert Frost. Reprinted by permission of Holt, Rinehart and Winston, Publishers.

To a Christmas Tree

Heaven twinkles where you stand
With the snow-drift in your hand
Interweaving myriad charms
As you cradle in your arms, —
Here a bauble — there a gem —
Little stars of Bethlehem!

Wistful now, and wonder-wise,
Children stand with lifted eyes
Gazing on your fair festoons
Of gossamer and magic moons,
Singing birds and swaying bells,
Marshmallows and caramels,
And every kind of fairy thing
That ornaments imagining.

Yuletide must be bare indeed
For him who feels no inner need
Of elfin dreams and elfin drums
Every year when Christmas comes.
He hears no goblin trumpets blow.
For him in vain the baubles glow
Who is so blind he cannot see
Beauty in a Christmas tree.

Mona Dale

Photo Opposite
THE WONDER OF CHRISTMAS
Three Lions

Little Lights of Christmas

A most charming Christmas custom from Spain has been adopted in many communities throughout the United States. "Little lights of Christmas" are decorating driveways and patios, stairways and rooftops. Called *luminarias*, these simple, lantern-type lights were used for centuries as the symbolic way to light the arrival of the Christ Child on Christmas Eve.

The custom originated in Spain where the first *luminarias* were bonfires made from crisscrossed pinon boughs built up into three-foot-high squares. When colored wrapping paper found its way to Spain from the Orient, people found it easier to use paper lanterns instead of bonfires. Gradually, the bonfires lost their popularity, and stringing colored lanterns through the trees or hanging them from wires around the house became the thing to do.

As Spanish people emigrated to Mexico, they brought the custom with them, and it spread throughout the Republic and into the southwestern United States, particularly New Mexico. In 1802, Yankee traders traveling down the Santa Fe Trail brought along brown paper bags, a new item among their supplies. It was then that paper bags replaced the colored lanterns, and they have been used ever since.

On Christmas Eve throughout New Mexico, entire villages are lit up only with *luminarias*. Every adobe hut, hacienda, sidewalk, and street is outlined with the festive lights, and every other light in town is turned off. The sight is so spectacular that thousands of people travel to New Mexico just to see the "little lights of Christmas." The city of Albuquerque has observed this tradition for more than thirty years. It is such an extravaganza that visitors to the city are picked up at their hotels by drivers who take them on a tour of the holiday fairyland.

Today *luminarias* are practical as well as symbolic when used to light the way for guests coming to holiday celebrations. Because they are so easy to make and because they conserve energy, they are ideal outdoor Christmas decorations.

To make *luminarias*, all you need are large grocery bags, a bucket of sand, and as many plumber's candles as you have grocery bags. Be sure that the bags have flat bottoms so they will stand up without leaning and will remain open. Then follow these three easy steps:

1. Fold down a two-inch cuff at the top of a grocery bag.
2. Fill the bag with two to three inches of sand.
3. Place a candle securely in the center of the sand.

Presto! You have a *luminaria*.

Luminarias are a wonderful Christmas custom for the whole family to enjoy. Even small children can fold down a cuff on the paper bag and help to pour in the sand. As the *luminaria* burns, there is no danger of fire because the flame is so far from the sides of the paper bag, and when the candle burns down far enough, the sand will extinguish the flame. With very little effort and expense, you can illuminate your home, conserve energy, and perpetuate a delightful Spanish tradition all at the same time.

At sunset on Christmas Eve, or anytime you're having a holiday party after dark, line your driveway, sidewalk, porch — even the rooftop, if you're young and daring, with "little lights of Christmas." Guests will be delighted with the glowing welcome, and what a charming way to light up the world at Christmastime. In some communities, entire neighborhoods join in the custom, turning a block or two of dark streets into a fantasy of lights —"little lights of Christmas!"

Vivian Buchan

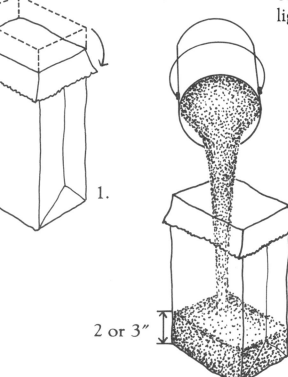

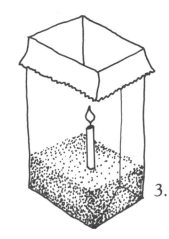

Away in a Manger

Away in a manger,
   No crib for a bed,
The little Lord Jesus
   Lay down His sweet head;
The stars in the sky
   Looked down where He lay,
The little Lord Jesus
   Asleep on the hay.

The cattle are lowing,
   The poor baby wakes,
But little Lord Jesus
   No crying He makes;
I love Thee, Lord Jesus!
   Look down from the sky,
And stay by my cradle
   Till morning is nigh.

Be near me, Lord Jesus,
   I ask Thee to stay
Close by me forever,
   And love me, I pray.
Bless all the dear children
   In thy tender care,
And take me to heaven
   To live with Thee there.

Anonymous

Photo Opposite
BABY JESUS
Three Lions

Christmas in Florida

The visitor sadly shook his head
As he baked in the tropical sun.
"Call this Christmas?" he said to me.
"Well, not where I come from.
Christmas needs snow and ice and cold,
And the sound of sleigh bells' ring.
And as for me I can't be sold
On weather that feels like spring."

We looked at him and then we smiled
As he scoffed at our awful plight.
And we felt pity and were not riled
'Cause he was so far from right.
For no snow fell on Bethlehem
On the night the star first shone.
There was no blizzard or howling gale
That swept with a shriek and a moan.

The breeze was soft and, what was more,
The night the Christ child came,
Hibiscus bloomed near the stable door
As Mary murmured His name.
Bougainvillea of violet hue,
Arched in a graceful bower;
Poinsettias wet with midnight dew
Enhanced that sacred hour.

The heavenly host in the starry sky
Proclaimed the birth of a king.
And rustling palms echoed the cry
As the whole earth seemed to sing.
So we find here in our sun-drenched land,
Untouched by ice and snow,
That the spirit of Christmas is at hand
And we feel God willed it so.

Author Unknown

O little town of Bethlehem,
  How still we see thee lie!
Above thy deep and dreamless sleep
  The silent stars go by.
Yet in thy dark streets shineth
  The everlasting Light;
The hopes and fears of all the years
  Are met in thee to-night.

The Innkeeper

Yes, they came to my inn at Bethlehem, and how well I remember the couple; it seems but yesterday. He was a manly sort of man, the kind that would cause you to look again if you saw him once; kindly and dignified, with long beard, a strong man with quiet manners. There was something that charmed me about the woman who was with him, and —well, I just can't tell you — anyway, one could see that she might soon become a mother. It rather worried me that I didn't have a place for them, but so many had come for the registration, you know. Sanballat, rich merchant, had come down from Damascus; Thaddeus, one of my old customers, had come up from Gaza. A party from Hebron came just at nightfall, and, since I knew them all, I could not turn them away. Joseph told me that he was from Nazareth, up in the hill country of Galilee. He thought, of course, he could have a place to stay, and, as he asked me, he looked toward Mary and knew that I would understand.

I did understand, and I tried to think which of the men I should ask to move and make place for the couple. But how could I ask these customers of mine to inconvenience themselves? After all, I did not know Joseph and Mary. I said to myself, O well, somebody will look after them; I must not disturb the others, and it is a beautiful star-lit night. Here, I have it, finally I said to myself, we can make room for them in the manger, and someway they will get along. I have wondered a lot about them since they have gone. He was a manly sort of man with his long beard and dignified look and quiet manners. And the woman, she was like a princess. I wish now that I had said to the men in my inn, "We must make a place for this man and this woman from Galilee!" But I didn't, and I am sorry. They might, after all, have been people of consequence.

Oliver M. Keve

Painting Opposite
NO ROOM AT THE INN
Robert A. Heuel

Prepare ye the way of the Lord, make straight in the desert a highway for our God. Ev'ry valley shall be exalted, and ev'ry mountain and hill made low; the crooked straight, and the rough places plain. And the glory of the Lord shall be revealed, and all flesh shall see it together, for the mouth of the Lord hath spoken it.

Isaiah 40:3-5

The Lord whom ye seek shall suddenly come to His temple, ev'n the messenger of the covenant, whom ye delight in; Behold, he shall come, saith the Lord of Hosts. But who may abide the day of His coming? And who shall stand when He appeareth?

Malachi 3:1-2

There were shepherds abiding in the field,
keeping watch over their flocks by night.
And lo! the angel of the Lord came upon
them and the glory of the Lord shone
round about them, and they were sore
afraid. And the angel said unto them,
"Fear not: for, behold, I bring you good
tidings of great joy, which shall be to all
people.

"For unto you is born this day in the city
of David a Savior, which is Christ the
Lord." And suddenly there was with the
angel a multitude of the heavenly host
praising God and saying: "Glory to God
in the highest, and peace on earth, good
will towards men."

Luke 2:8-11,13,14

That Night's Glory

Softly sibilant, through the night
Was heard the sound of angels' flight.
Earthward they came on shining wings
Telling the shepherds of wondrous things;
    And all was light
    On Christmas night.

There in that cold and barren field
With golden voices they revealed
God's marvelous plan: the Messiah's birth
Bringing redemption to all the earth:
    And all was light
    On Christmas night.

Between the earth and heaven that night
Was set a star to mark the site
Where in a manger God sent down
A heavenly King without a crown
    Who brought the light
    On Christmas night.

The angels are silent; the star is gone,
Yet that night's glory lingers on
Within the hearts of all who love
The Savior sent us from above;
    And all is light.
    Each Christmas night.

Mina Morris Scott

Painting Opposite
SHEPHERDS IN THE FIELD
Robert A. Heuel

All we like sheep have gone astray, we have turned ev'ry one to his own way; and the Lord hath laid on Him the iniquity of us all.

Isaiah 53:6

He shall feed His flock like a shepherd, and He shall gather the lambs with His arm and carry them in His bosom, and gently lead those that are with young.

Isaiah 40:11

*For unto us a Child is born, unto us a
Son is given: and the government shall
be upon his shoulder; and his Name shall
be called Wonderful Counselor, The
mighty God, The everlasting Father, The
Prince of Peace.*

Isaiah 9:6

*Come unto Him, all ye that labour, come
unto Him, ye that are heavy laden, and
He will give you rest.*

Matthew 11:28

First Christmas

The stars up in the midnight skies
Shone warm and clear and bright
When Christ was born in Bethlehem
Upon that holy night.

They shone with glory on the stall
Wherein the Baby lay
In Mary's arms, in swaddling clothes,
Upon the fragrant hay.

The cattle gazed with wondering eyes
But did not think it odd
To see the Little One with them —
He was the Lamb of God.

And Joseph looked with loving eyes
Upon the both of them;
It was a wondrous, beautiful,
Still night in Bethlehem.

Roy Z. Kemp

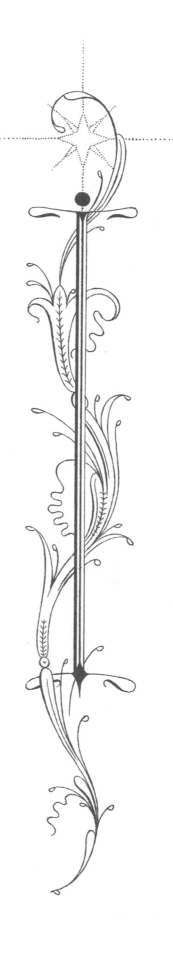

Painting Opposite
JOSEPH
Robert A. Heuel

*Rejoice greatly, O daughter of Zion!
Shout, O daughter of Jerusalem: behold,
thy king cometh unto thee; He is the
righteous Savior.*

Zechariah 9:9,10

*O thou that tellest good tidings to Zion,
get thee up into the high mountain! O
thou that tellest good tidings to
Jerusalem, lift up thy voice with strength!
Lift it up, be not afraid! Say unto the
cities of Judah, Behold your God!*

Isaiah 40:9

Hallelujah! Hallelujah!
Hallelujah! Hallelujah! Hallelujah!
For the Lord God Omnipotent reigneth...
And He shall reign for ever and ever.

Revelations 19:6; 11:15

King of Kings, for ever and ever.
Hallelujah! Hallelujah!
And Lord of Lords, for ever and ever.
Hallelujah! Hallelujah!
And he shall reign for ever and ever.

Revelations 19:6, 16

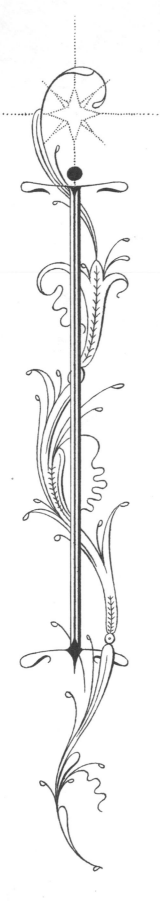

Christmas Questions

Did only wise men see the light
That glimmered from the star that night?
Did only shepherds hear the song
That drifted from the angel throng?

Who knows, my child, or who will tell?
I only know, and know it well,
That those who look upon the high
And soundless avenues of sky,
Who yearn to see a new star gleaming
See things beyond their deepest dreaming;

That folk as lowly as the sod
Will often hear the choirs of God,
And *all* who seek the manger place
Will see the Child's sweet holy face.

Grace V. Watkins

Painting Opposite
COME TO THE MANGER
Robert A. Heuel

Emily Carey Alleman

In 1957, Emily Carey Alleman published a book of poetry entitled *The Gypsy Heart*, and indeed, for twenty-six years of her life, this best-loved poet was a veritable gypsy.

Emily was born in Indiana in 1893. She spent her early years in Oklahoma where her father homesteaded 160 acres when the Indian Territory first opened to settlers. In 1906, her family moved to Canada and, in 1912, moved again to southern California. It was 1919 before Emily finally settled in Santa Ana, California with her husband, Herbert Alleman. She still lives there today, and she still, at age ninety-one, writes her poetry.

Emily's poems have been widely published in magazines, books and newspapers. Hallmark Cards, Inc. has purchased the greeting card rights to poems in *The Gypsy Heart* and, to date, has used the material in over 100 cards and booklets.

Although she has lost most of her eyesight, Emily still has insight when it comes to people and nature. Such insight is evident in her extensive collection of Christmas poems, many of which grace the more than 500 Christmas cards she sends and receives each year.

The Night Before Christmas

It must be a wearisome thing to be
A little, leftover Christmas tree —
To stand out on a vacant lot,
Unwanted, unloved, alone, forgot;
To have your dearest dream snuffed out,
Your fondest wishes put to rout.

When you were cut from your place in the sun,
I know you hoped to delight someone —
To be a symbol of the Christ Child's birth,
To be surrounded by joy and mirth,
To wear twinkling lights, have stars in your hair,
Proclaim God's love just by being there.

O little, leftover Christmas tree,
There still is time. *Come home with me!*

Our Christmas Prayer

Dear Lord, in humbleness we pray
For Thy firm guidance, day by day.

Help us to know the right from wrong,
To greet each morning with a song.

Let Thy people everywhere
Know that we are glad to share.

Bless their homes, Lord, bless their land!
Help us all to understand

The problems that our neighbors face —
The problems of the human race.

Bring Joy and Peace to all mankind,
Let good will travel unconfined.

I Sought the Path to Christmas

I journeyed once on a wintry way
To seek the path where Christmas lay.

I saw the glow of a distant star,
Heard temple bells, both near and far.

I followed the mirthful song of laughter;
When beauty fled, I hurried after.

I trudged, foot-sore, up a rocky hill —
The night was long; the air was still.

I knelt to warm a frozen bird;
I shared my bread where hunger stirred.

I gave love's gift — saw hope's dream start,
And I found Christmas in my heart.

What Is Christmas?

"What is Christmas?" I asked the child.
"It's the happiest day of the year!
When Jesus was born, when bells are rung,
When Santa Claus comes and carols are sung,"
The child replied.

"What is Christmas?" I asked a mother.
"It's the tenderest day of the year!
When homefolk and friends seem somehow dearer,
When hearts grow closer, when Heaven comes nearer,"
The mother said.

"What is Christmas?" I asked an old man.
"It's the holiest day of the year!
When men forget self and think of others,
When love's deep bond makes all men brothers,"
The old one said.

My Gift to You

I took the song of a meadowlark,
The velvet hush of early dark,
The music of rain, the laugh of a child,
The peal of bells — now soft, now wild;

I took the peace of the morning star,
A spice-scented breeze from Zanzibar,
The loveliness of a half-blown rose,
The piquant charm of scarlet bows

And hung them high on your Christmas tree,
Where no one at all could possibly see,
And no one at all will know —
But me!

Our Gift to Him

Come, let us go, you and I,
Through the starless night,
Through the wind, through the rain,
To ease the foundling's cry of pain,
To bring to old concerns warm sun,
Bring friendship's solace to the lonely one.

Come, let us go, you and I.
Let the burdened of heart know we really care,
Not by wishing them well but by being there;
And, when the glad bells of Christmas ring,
May "love for others" be our gift to Him.

Come, let us go, you and I!

I Heard the Bells on Christmas Day

I heard the bells on Christmas Day
Their old, familiar carols play,
And wild and sweet
The words repeat
Of peace on earth, good will to men!

I thought how, as the day had come,
The belfries of all Christendom
Had rolled along
The unbroken song
Of peace on earth, good will to men!

And in despair I bowed my head:
"There is no peace on earth," I said,
"For hate is strong
And mocks the song
Of peace on earth, good will to men."

Then pealed the bells more loud and deep:
"God is not dead; nor doth he sleep!
The wrong shall fail
The right prevail,
With peace on earth, good will to men!"

Henry Wadsworth Longfellow

Photo Opposite
CHRISTMAS BELLS
Bob Coyle

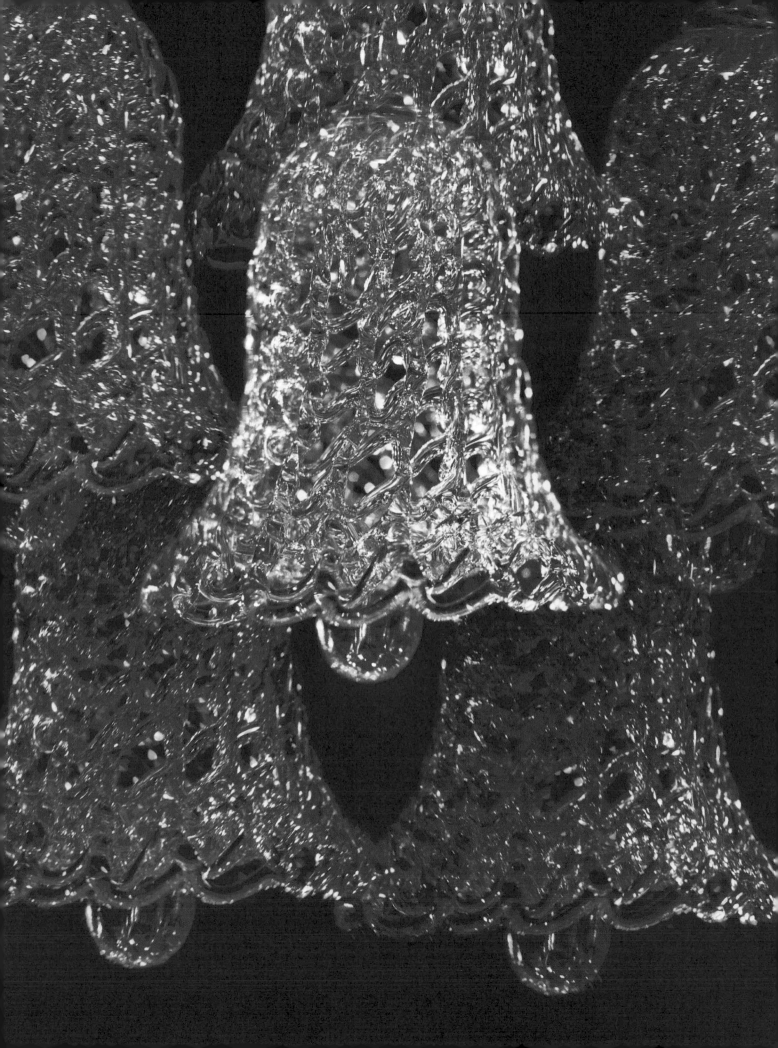

'Tis Christmas

'Tis a day for the children,
For laughter and fun
From the early light's dawning
'Til the last carol's sung.

'Tis a wide-eyed enchantment
To see the great tree
And the gifts Santa's left there
For you and for me.

'Tis a time to browse over
The gay Christmas cards
With their sentiments swelling
The best of regards.

'Tis the day that the turkey
Will taste best of all,
When our dear friends and neighbors
Drop in to call.

'Tis a landscape bedecked with
Soft blankets of white;
'Tis a sparkle and glitter
From morning 'til night.

Georgia B. Adams

Christmas Love

I woke up early Christmas morn,
Before the sun had kissed the dawn;
I stood before the Christmas tree
And eyed its beauty quietly.

Its branches held some silver chains
And lollipops and candy canes,
And there were brightly-colored lights —
Even little handmade kites.

Teddy bears and dolls that cry,
A rocking horse with head held high —
Presents wrapped so lovingly
Waited 'neath the sparkling tree.

Then, the rush of tiny feet
Made my Christmas morn complete;
Sounds of laughter 'round me flew
And made my Christmas dream come true.

A lovely pair of bright blue eyes
Smiled with wonder and surprise.
This day's the best one of the year
Especially since a child lives here.

Patricia Emme

Two Dresses

"I'm tired of this dark green dress,"
Miss Evergreen complained.
"I've worn it for a long time.
It's shabby now and stained."

Then winter came with cold north winds
And brought a sparkling gown
Of diamonds on snowy white,
With crystals hanging down.

Miss Evergreen shook out her skirt,
And, with a happy cry,
She looked around and proudly said,
"Two dresses now have I."

Jean Reedy

Uncle Santa

My childhood's great ambition
Was frustrated because
I couldn't get Aunt Mary
To marry Santa Claus.

With Santa for an uncle,
I reckoned to become
The envy of all other kids
Throughout all Christendom.

A story-telling maiden aunt
And dearly loved was she —
A perfect mate for Santa,
But she thought differently!

She said, "He simply will not do.
His beard would make a mess
When he ate soup; and I will not
Endure such sloppiness;

And furthermore, if you don't stop
This wearisome pursuit,
I'll booby-trap the chimney —
I'll fix that darned old coot!"

So Santa's not my uncle.
In fact, as I recall,
He's never shown himself to be
Much kin to me at all,

But, for the youngsters of today
I have some sound advice:
This coming crop of aunties
Thinks beards are very nice.

So one of *you* might snag him
For an uncle, if you try,
And I sincerely hope that you
Have better luck than I!

Ruth Van Gorder

Secrets

We have a secret, Mommy and me;
We're just as clever as we can be.
We're knitting Daddy a pair of socks,
And we're going to wrap them in a box
That we will tie with ribbons gay —
But he won't get them till Christmas Day!

We have a secret, Daddy and me;
We're just as jolly as we can be.
We're giving Mommy a bright new locket
That I have hidden right here in my pocket.
Oh, I can't wait to hear what she'll say,
When she opens her present on Christmas Day!

We have a secret, just we three;
We're buying baby a Christmas tree.
We're going to trim it with ornaments bright,
And all of its branches will glitter with light.
But it's a secret, so I won't say
A thing about it till Christmas Day!

Mommy and Daddy whisper and sigh;
They've just hidden something away up high,
And I'm as happy as I can be
'Cause I know it's a secret just for me!
So, I won't even ask to play
With whatever-it-is until Christmas Day!

Jean Dundas Webb

The Art of Gift Giving

by A. A. Milne

To Angela,
From Father
and William

And now I am reminded of the ingenuity of a friend of mine, William by name, who arrived at a large country house for Christmas without any present in his bag. He had expected neither to give nor to receive anything, but to his horror he discovered on the 24th that everybody was preparing a Christmas present for him, and that it was taken for granted that he would require a little privacy and brown paper on Christmas Eve for the purpose of addressing his own offerings to others. He had wild thoughts of telegraphing to London for something to be sent down, and spoke to other members of the house-party in order to discover what sort of presents would be suitable.

"What are you giving our host?" he asked....

"Mary and I are giving him a book," said John, referring to his wife.

William then approached the youngest son of the house, and discovered that he and his next brother Dick were sharing in this, that, and the other. When he had heard this, William retired to his room and thought profoundly.

He was the first down to breakfast on Christmas morning. All the places at the table were piled high with presents. He looked at John's place. The top parcel said, "To John and Mary from Charles." William took out his fountain-pen and added a couple of words to the inscription. It then read, "To John and Mary from Charles and William," and in William's opinion looked just as effective as before. He moved on to the next place. "To Angela from Father," said the top parcel. "And William," wrote William.

At his hostess' place he hesitated for a moment. The first present there was for "Darling Mother, from her loving children." It did not seem that an "and William" was quite suitable. But his hostess was not to be deprived of William's kindly thought, twenty seconds later the handkerchiefs "from John and Mary and William" expressed all the nice things which he was feeling for her. He passed on to the next place....

It is of course impossible to thank every donor of a joint gift; one simply thanks the first person whose eye one happens to catch. Sometimes William's eye was caught, sometimes not. But he was spared all embarrassment; and I can recommend his solution of the problem with perfect confidence to those who may be in a similar predicament....

From IF I MAY by A. A. Milne. Copyright 1921 by E. P. Dutton, renewed 1949 by A. A. Milne. Reprinted by permission of the publisher, E. P. Dutton, a division of New American Library.

Hooray! Hooray!
for Christmas Day
and Christmas trees
so bright and gay.
Though sad the trees
soon disappear,
the gifts beneath may
last for years!

D. L. Gibbs

Art by Rick Reinert from *The Nutcracker*, adapted from E.T.A. Hoffmann, retold by Ron Kidd, copyright 1985 by Ideals Publishing Corporation. *The Nutcracker* is available in hardcover edition through Ideals Publishing Corporation, Nelson Place at Elm Hill Pike, Nashville, Tennessee 37214 (615-889-9000). Price: $5.95 plus $1.00 postage and handling.

Gifts from Auntie

Everyone gives me such sensible stuff,
Such practical presents of which I've enough,
Except Auntie, who seems to believe in surprises
Whenever a special occasion arises.

Her packages always are tempting and gay:
A fancy fur muffler, a pink negligee;
One time, a gilt-bordered album of rhymes,
The next time, a powder box fashioned with chimes.

Pajamas and sweaters and stockings and gloves
Are all very welcome, but gee, a girl loves
Some other small luxuries reason might bar,
And Auntie seems, somehow, to know what they are.

Mary Shirley Krouse

Just for Little Boys?

My husband stood and watched the train
That ran around the track.
His rapt expression made it plain
Its journey moved him back
Along the route of many years
To when he was a boy
And in the ranks of engineers
That guided such a toy.

The little boxcars didn't know
How full of thought their load.
The red caboose would never show
The stowaway who rode
And followed every dip and climb.
Who says the world of toys
(Especially at Christmastime)
Is just for little boys?

Margaret Rorke

Christmas in Toyland

The soldiers marched in a gay parade,
Happy the tunes their little band played.
Small plastic dolls with fluttering eyes
Looked at the soldiers with great surprise,
While the china dolls stood on a shelf,
Each one a beauty, proud of herself,
And the other dolls, all dressed in style,
Showed the latest of fashions with a smile.

A jack-in-the-box bounced up and down,
Stealing some laughs from Bobo, the clown.
Lions and tigers, pandas and bears,
Danced about with turtles and hares,
While Cathy, the cat, and Fido, the dog,
Joined in a song with Jumpy, the frog.
Zippo, the monkey, waved a small mop,
And, off in a corner, there spun a top.

King Thor and Queen Anne, on the castle wall,
Were laughing and having themselves a ball,
While the prince and princess danced with the toys.
Fiddlers played on in spite of the noise,
And Santa Claus sat with pipe aglow,
A jolly old gent. How he loved the show!
At Christmas, in Toyland, such scenes you'll view.
Enjoy it, children, it's all for you.

Anton J. Stoffle

Photo Opposite
CHRISTMAS JOYS
Three Lions

There's nothing Santa
 more enjoys
Than making toys for
 girls and boys,
And in his way he's
 wondrous wise,
For he knows just
 what'll please
Your eyes.

The Way It Used to Be

Robert Benchley was on a diet when he read an old menu for a Christmas dinner served to the guests of a famous Chicago hotel in 1885. He expressed his envious amazement as follows...

Whe you bought a dinner in those days, you bought a *dinner*. None of this skimming over the card and saying, "I don't see anything I want. Just bring me an alligator-pear salad." If you couldn't see anything you wanted on one of the old-fashioned table d'hote menus, you just couldn't see, that's all...

After the customary blue-points and soup, with a comparatively meager assortment of fish (just a stuffed black bass and boiled salmon), we find a choice of broiled leg of mountain sheep or wild turkey. This is just as a starter. The boys didn't get down to business until the roast. There are thirty-six choices among the roasts. Among the more distinguished names listed were:

Leg of moose, loin of elk, cinnamon bear, blacktail deer, loin of venison, saddle of antelope (the National Geographic Society evidently did the shopping for meat in behalf of this hotel), opossum, black bear, and then the duck.

The duck will have to have a paragraph all by itself. In fact, we may have to build a small house for it. When this chef came to the duck, he just threw his apron over his head and said: "I'm going crazy, boys — don't stop me!" He had canvasback duck, wood duck, butterball duck, brant, mallard duck, blue-winged teal, spoonbill duck, sage hen, green-winged teal, and pintail duck, to say nothing of partridge, quail, plover, and some other of the cheap birds...

...So, after toying with all the members of the duck family except decoys and clay pigeons, the diner of 1885 cast his eye down the card to what were called "Broiled," a very simple, honest name for what followed. Teal duck (evidently one of the teal ducks from the roast column slipped down into the broiled, and liked it so well that it stayed), ricebirds, marshbirds, sand snipe, reedbirds, blackbirds, and red-winged starling...

By this time you would have supposed that they had used up all the birds within a radius of 3,000 miles of Chicago, leaving none to wake people up in the morning. But no. Among the entrées they must have a fillet of pheasant *financiere*, which certainly must have come as a surprise to the dinner parties and tasted good after all that broiled pheasant and roast pheasant. Nothing tastes so good after a broiled pheasant as a good fillet of pheasant *financiere*...

There then seemed to have come over the chef a feeling that he wasn't doing quite the right thing by his guests. Oh, it had been all right up to this point, but he hadn't really shown what he could do. So he got up a team of what he called "ornamental dishes," and when he said "ornamental" I rather imagine he meant "ornamental." They probably had to be brought in by the town fire department and eaten standing on a ladder. Playing left end for the "ornamental dishes" we find a pyramid of wild turkey in aspic. Perhaps you would like to stop right there. If you did you would miss the aspic of lobster Queen Victoria, and you couldn't really be said to have dined unless you had had aspic of lob-ster Queen Victoria. I rather imagine that it made quite an impressive ornamental dish — that is, if it looked anything like Queen Victoria...

Now the question arises — what did people look like after they had eaten a dinner like that? Were people in 1885 so much fatter than those of us today who go around nibbling at bits of pineapple and drinking sips of sauer-kraut juice? I personally don't remember, but it doesn't seem that people were so much worse off in those days. At any rate, they had a square meal once in a while.

I am not a particularly proud man and it doesn't make an awful lot of difference to anyone whether I am fat or not. But as I don't like to run out of breath when I stoop over to tie my shoes, I try to follow the various bits of advice which people give me in the matter of diet. As a result, I get very little to eat, and am cross and hungry most of the time. I feel like a crook every time I take a furtive forkful of potato, and once, after sneaking a piece of hot bread, I was on the verge of giving myself up to the police as a dangerous character.

Surely there are more noble aspects (aspect of lobster Queen Victoria, for instance) than that of a man who is afraid to take a piece of bread. I am going to get some photographs of people in 1885 and give quite a lot of study to finding out whether they were very much heavier than people today. If I find that they weren't, I am going to take that menu of the Chicago Christmas dinner and get some chef, or organization of chefs, to duplicate it. The worst that can happen to me after eating it will be that I drop dead.

Robert Benchley

From CHIPS OFF THE OLD BENCHLEY by Robert Benchley. Copyright 1949 by Gertrude D. Benchley. Reprinted by permission of Harper & Row, Publishers, Inc.

Christmas Delights

Old-Fashioned Fruitcake
Makes one 10-inch cake

1 pound raisins
1 pound currants
8 ounces candied cherries, chopped; reserve
    4 whole cherries for garnish
8 ounces candied yellow, red, and green
    pineapple
2 ounces candied lemon peel
2 ounces candied orange peel
6 ounces grated coconut
4 ounces walnuts, chopped
¼ cup chopped pecans

¾ cup flour
½ teaspoon allspice
½ teaspoon ground cloves
½ teaspoon nutmeg
½ teaspoon ground cinnamon
¼ teaspoon salt
½ pound unsalted butter, softened
¾ cup sugar
6 large eggs
½ cup apple juice
Whole pecans for garnish

Grease and flour a 10-inch tube pan. Place waxed paper on bottom of pan; set aside. In a very large bowl, combine raisins, currants, cherries, pineapple, lemon peel, orange peel, coconut, walnuts, and pecans. In a separate small bowl, mix flour, spices, and salt; gradually blend into fruit mixture, coating fruit well. In another bowl, cream butter and sugar until light and fluffy. Beat in eggs, one at a time. Beat in apple juice. Combine butter mixture with fruit and flour mixture; blend well. Pour batter into prepared baking pan. Preheat oven to 225°; place broiler pan with water on bottom rack of oven. Put cake on a low rack just above the water; bake for 4 to 4½ hours or until a toothpick inserted in cake comes out clean. Cool cake in pan; invert onto a baking rack. Keep cake wrapped tightly in plastic and foil until serving time. Before serving, garnish with reserved cherries and whole pecans.

Figgy Pudding
Makes 12 to 16 servings

½ cup unsalted butter, softened
1½ cups dark brown sugar
2 large eggs
1 teaspoon vanilla
1 teaspoon rum extract
1 cup finely chopped apple
1 cup seedless raisins
½ cup coarsely chopped walnuts

4 ounces candied lemon peel, chopped
4 ounces candied orange peel, chopped
1 cup flour
1 teaspoon baking soda
½ teaspoon salt
2 teaspoons cinnamon
1 teaspoon ground cloves
1 cup fine dry bread crumbs

In a large mixing bowl, cream butter and brown sugar using an electric mixer. Beat in eggs, vanilla, and rum extract; blend well. Stir in apple, raisins, walnuts, lemon peel, and orange peel; blend well. In a separate bowl, combine flour, baking soda, salt, and spices; stir into batter. Add bread crumbs and blend. Pack mixture into a greased 1½-quart mold; leave 1 inch of space at top of mold. Cover mold tightly and place on a rack in a large kettle. Pour boiling water into kettle to a depth halfway up the outside of the mold. Cover kettle; cook over high heat until water steams. Reduce heat; continue steaming for 3 hours. Remove mold from kettle; let stand 10 minutes. Unmold pudding; cool completely on a rack. Wrap cooled pudding tightly in foil; refrigerate or freeze for several days to blend flavors. At serving time, warm wrapped pudding in a 350° oven or resteam.

Photo Opposite
CHRISTMAS DELIGHTS
Index Stone

Interlude

The week that follows Christmas
Is to me the best of all;
The rushing days are over
And friends have time to call.

What joy to read the greetings
Beside the lighted tree;
What pleasure now to travel
The miles of memories.

The week that follows Christmas
Holds restfulness and cheer;
It's a time for meditation
At the closing of the year.

Hilda Butler Farr

Come Dream with Me

Come sit beside my fireside, friend,
The lights are glowing there,
And there's a log that's burning bright
To warm the winter air,
A heart that's kind and helpful, too,
So sure to understand,
And always, in the evening cool,
A warm and friendly hand.

Come sit with me and dream, my dear,
While twilight fades away.
We've memories we two can share
This happy time of day.
We'll watch the shadows of the night,
Upon the ceiling dim,
And find a smile in tender thoughts
That we can live again.

Garnett Ann Schultz

Photo Opposite
HOT CIDER
H. Armstrong Roberts

Where All Is Warm and Gay

Today the winds are cold and drear,
The ground is white with snow;
And o'er the landscape far and near —
Wherever people go —
I hear them worry and complain.
To keep their bodies warm,
They battle with the winds in vain,
Weak victims of the storm.

But oh, what comfort comes to me,
What courage drives me on!
My spirit bids all worries flee
And every care be gone.
Let fury rage! It shall not chill
The little home that waits for me,
Where those I love keep watch until
My eager face once more they see.

O. Lawrence Hawthorne

Grandpa Wore
a Stocking Cap

"Stocking caps are made for boys,"
Is what my Grandpa said.
And every winter he would wear
A warm one on his head.

Mother heard him tell me so,
And she knew what to do.
If stocking caps warmed Grandpa's ears,
Then I must have one too.

Now all the other boys I know
Wear ear muffs or a hat.
And some boys go bareheaded,
But Mother scorns at that.

So, when the wind blew brisk and cold,
She took me into town
And fitted caps, then curtly said,
"I guess we'll take the brown."

Elva Horton Weber

Overleaf
WINTER'S SPARKLE
Index Stone

Country Chronicle

How brilliantly the stars gleam and glisten on sharp December nights! A man regards the sky at this time of year as a lighted Christmas tree illuminating the heavens for all to see. The sparkling and shining high overhead are akin to strands of twinkling ornaments on the bending boughs of the spruce or the pine. Whether the land sleeps under the snowy quilt of a northern wintertime or rests beneath a carpet of autumn's fallen leaves in the foothills of the Blue Ridge, the skies are the same — and so are the stars.

It seems that the stars are always brighter and more luminous when the sharp cold has brushed away the haze that so often shrouds the atmosphere on warmer, milder days. Gazing at the display, one well may envision those ages past when the Wise Men followed the Star in the East to the manger where the

Christ-child was born nearly two thousand years ago. A man would have the stars shine as symbols of the miracle in Bethlehem, a reminder of Christ's birth and His enduring gift of love; a gift to be cherished and shared through the ages, from one generation to another; a love rekindled each December as we joyously celebrate the anniversary of His birth.

Christmas bestows upon mankind cheer and inspiration from the songs of carolers wending their way through the streets of cities and hamlets to the hymns and homilies pouring from the pulpits and choir lofts of churches throughout the land. Let the bells and carols and the message of Christmas flow freely in praise of Him whose endowment to mankind is our heritage without end!

Lansing Christman

Reflections of Grandeur

Purple shadows on the snow,
Dying embers fade and glow —
Majestic calm of winter's night
Makes a heavy heart feel light.

Gifts of love were sent to me,
Some with bows tied tenderly,
But, somewhere in this silent night,
God's pure love is shining bright

Like the star that cast its glow
Above the manger long ago.
Now ornaments that trim the tree
Reflect the grandeur silently.

Christmastide's an incarnation
Of God's love for every nation.

Clay Harrison

Photo Opposite
DENVER CIVIC CENTER
H. Armstrong Roberts

Well, So That Is That...

Well, so that is that.
Now we must dismantle the tree,
Putting the decorations back
    into their cardboard boxes —
Some have got broken —
And carrying them up to the attic.
The holly and mistletoe must be taken down
    and burnt,
And the children got ready for school.
There are enough left-overs to do,
    warmed up, for the rest of the week —
Not that we have much appetite, having
    drunk such a lot, stayed up so late,
    attempted — quite unsuccessfully —
To love all our relatives, and in general
Grossly overestimated our powers.
Once again as in previous years we have seen
    the actual Vision and failed
To do more than entertain it as an agreeable
Possibility, once again we have sent Him away
Begging though to remain His disobedient
    servant,
The promising child who cannot keep
    His word for long.

W. H. Auden

Copyright 1944 by W. H. Auden. Excerpt reprinted from "For the Time Being: A Christmas Oratorio" in W. H. AUDEN: COLLECTED POEMS, edited by Edward Mendelson, by permission of Random House, Inc. and Faber & Faber Ltd., London.

A flower unblown; a book unread;
A tree with fruit unharvested;
A path untrod; a house whose rooms
Lack yet the heart's divine perfumes —
This is the year that for you waits
Beyond tomorrow's mystic gates.

Horatio Nelson Powers

ACKNOWLEDGMENTS

O LITTLE TOWN OF BETHLEHEM by Phillips Brooks; FLOWER OF THE HOLY NIGHT from CHRISTMAS IN THE HEART by Della Adams Leitner; CHRISTMAS IN FLORIDA submitted by Beatrice M. Lovelace; COME DREAM WITH ME from THE LITTLE THINGS by Garnett Ann Schultz, copyright © 1964 by Dorrance & Company; CHRISTMAS CLOCKS and UNCLE SANTA from CHRISTMAS, copyright © 1985 by Ruth Van Gorder; CHRISTMAS QUESTIONS by Grace V. Watkins originally printed in *War Cry*, December, 1960; GRANDPA WORE A STOCKING CAP by Elva Horton Weber reprinted with permission of Gary Weber. Our sincere thanks to the following people whose addresses we were unable to locate: Mona Dale for TO A CHRISTMAS TREE from YOUNG IN HEART, copyright © 1967 by Nancy R. Patterson; Mr. Edward Hawthorne for CHRISTMAS by O. Lawrence Hawthorne; Mrs. Oliver M. Keve for THE INNKEEPER by Oliver M. Keve; Horatio Nelson Powers for "A flower unblown..."; and Jean Dundas Webb for SECRETS.

ADDITIONAL PHOTOGRAPH/ART ACKNOWLEDGMENTS

Inside front and back cover photographs by Gene Ahrens. Painting of rocking horse by John M. Druckenmiller.

*MERRY CHRISTMAS AND
BEST WISHES FOR THE NEW YEAR
FROM ALL OF US AT IDEALS*